ANCIENT
SYSTEMOLOGY

POCKET EDITION

Published from
Mardukite Borsippa HQ, San Luis Valley, Colorado
Mardukite Academy & Systemology Society
for spiritual or educational purposes only

ANCIENT SYSTEMOLOGY

WISDOM OF
THE ARCANE TABLETS

A Basic Course developed
by Joshua Free
for the Systemology Society

THE JOSHUA FREE IMPRINT
JFI PUBLICATIONS

© 2023, JOSHUA FREE

ISBN : 978-1-961509-21-4

Also available in hardcover as
"Fundamentals of Systemology"

Pocket Paperback Edition — *October 2023*

mardukite.com

SYSTEMOLOGY is the
"New Thought" of the 21st Century.

It is the study of how
Spiritual Beings with unlimited power
became entrapped in the
Human Condition.

This study is an applied philosophy
— "A Pathway to Ascension" —
that charts our way back out,
freeing the True Self to experience
higher levels of existence again.

Systemology is the true science of the
"Matrix."

After more than a decade of
development, the "Fundamentals of
Systemology" are concisely explored
here in the first official
"Basic Course" on the subject ever
given by Joshua Free for the
Mardukite Academy.

It's time to discover
who you really are...
because you
were never "Human."

Fundamentals of Systemology
Basic Course Lesson Booklets

Lesson #1
BEING MORE THAN HUMAN
Rediscovering the Spiritual Self

Lesson #2
REALITIES IN AGREEMENT
Spiritual Life and The Universe

Lesson #3
WINDOWS TO EXPERIENCE
The Filters of Human Perception

Lesson #4
ANCIENT SYSTEMOLOGY
Wisdom From the Arcane Tablets

Lesson #5
A HISTORY OF SYSTEMOLOGY
Evolution of a Spiritual Science

Lesson #6
SYSTEMOLOGY PROCESSING
Practices of Spiritual Awakening

TABLET OF CONTENTS

INTRODUCTION
TO THE
"BASIC COURSE"

WELCOME, SEEKER!
YOUR JOURNEY ON THE PATHWAY
BEGINS HERE

This is a basic course in *Systemology*—specifically, the fundamental principles of *Mardukite Systemology*.

Quite simply: *Mardukite Systemology* is a new evolution in Human understanding about the "systems" governing *Spiritual Life*, *Reality*, the *Universe* and all *Existences*.

In many ways, *Systemology* is a 21st Century breakthrough that continues the legacy—and unifies the original pursuits—of early 20th Century *"American New Thought"* and other metaphysical schools of philosophy and mysticism. These are mostly all generalized (and often dismissed) in modern culture as *"New Age"* beliefs, though they are actually quite *"old"*—some even based on the most ancient known writings of discovered civilizations.

Mardukite Systemology was once concisely described as "an applied spiritual technology of the 21st Century A.D., based on spiritual wisdom from the 21st Century B.C." because of our use of *"Mesopotamian" Arcane Tablets* as source material for its foundations (and from which it retains a *"Mardukite"* designation).

The original *New Thought Movement* in America applied a "Western Civilization" approach to "Eastern" concepts—concepts that we now take for granted today, but of which were relatively unknown to the general population at that time. The movement sought to develop an "applied spiritual philosophy" whereby an individual could unlock their hidden potentials, untapped *"Knowingness"* and higher spiritual states of *Beingness*. These innate or native conditions of *Self* (as a *Spirit*) are blocked—or "fragmented"—by a "human" preoccupation with identifying *Self* as one and the same with the material body that it is merely using as a "vehicle" to experience (communicate and interact) within *this* Physical Universe.

Early *New Thought* work primarily emphasized practical "healing" applications (*mental healing, faith healing, &tc.*)—but at its very core, we may restate the ultimate pursuit or original focus was to "free humans *to be* their ideal native spiritual state."

This goal has been with us—lingering on the periphery of the "surface world"—for much longer than the existence of a *New Thought Movement*. In fact, for as long as "spiritual beings" have found themselves entrapped by a "Human Condition" and enforced to experience *this* "material existence" (fragmented from their true *Self*), a continuing pursuit has ensued to correct the situation—at least by those individuals still retaining enough *Awareness* to realize it.

Humans have been figuring on how to break free from the *"Matrix"* for a very long time. The desire or ambition to rise above the "standard-issue" Human Condition is already there. But the truth is that many other remotely similar "evolutions" of *New Thought* have dissolved into "multi-level marketing" schemes, "motivational pop-psychology" coaching, abusive "cult-like" movements—or heavily promoted books that skyrocket to the peaks of literary "bestseller lists" only to be discarded soon after and forgotten. They all share one thing in common: they all seem to capitalize on an innate desire or yearning we have to *"ascend"*—but, of course, without delivering stable results.

Even the most pious and well-meaning

philosophies and spiritual sciences have each fallen short of piercing the *"invisible barriers"* of perception separating *this* "Physical Universe" from any other "higher" existence—and with it, blocking our "way out" and the *Awareness* of our own true native state as an *Eternal Spirit*.

SYSTEMOLOGY:
21ST CENTURY NEW THOUGHT

Our *Systemology* is a new approach to *"Self-Actualization"*—completely relevant for the modern age and the future—and quite different from previous attempts or other traditions you might find.

Former attempts at overcoming *"barriers"* or *"gates"* of *reality* have included simply pretending that they don't exist, rejecting all material existence—all *time* and *space* —as an *"illusion"* and consequently losing the ability to actually *confront* the *reality* of anything *"As-It-Is."*

Our *Systemology* is also the answer to the "great mysteries" pervading the material sciences and natural philosophies; for they only seek to further qualify and validate the *reality agreements* made for *this* Physical Universe—and thus their level of understanding can never successfully pass the "barriers" either.

When applying our philosophy and techniques, the "systematic routes" outlined for an individual to increase their *"Actualized Awareness"* (and reach gradually higher toward their *"Spiritual Ascension"*) is referred to as *"The Pathway"*—and we call that individual a *"Seeker."*

At the start of *The Pathway*, early *routes* emphasize establishing a strong personal foundation of emotional well-being and mental strength before a *Seeker* is introduced to more advanced exercises and practices.

As a *Seeker* increases their *Awareness* in this lifetime, their spiritual "*Knowingness*" also increases—which is to say their sense of "*certainty*"; a certainty on *Life*, on this and other *Universes*, but more accurately, an increased certainty on *Self* as a practically unlimited "spiritual being" *having* an enforced restrictive "human experience."

One of the goals of "*Systematic Processing*" techniques in *Systemology* is to increase the ability of a *Seeker* to actually control and direct the "*attention*" of *Self* as a "spiritual being"—and as a result, *knowingly* increase command of the "human experience." This is a part of what we mean by "*Actualized Awareness*."

THREE STATES OF KNOWINGNESS

Raising a *Seeker's* level of *Actualized Awareness* requires, by definition, "bringing what is *hidden* (or not consciously known) up into the realm of *light* or *Knowingness*." We might go as far to say, as an imperfect example, that there are three primary states of *Knowingness*: *actual knowing*, *almost knowing* and *not-knowing*.

Actual knowing is what an individual is conscious of and can easily recall as needed. It makes up our "surface" (or "above-the-surface") thoughts; what is *"actually known"* and available to *Self* for "inspection" or analytical thought. This includes what we have *certainty* on as part of our *reality*.

Then, there are other *things* "below-the-

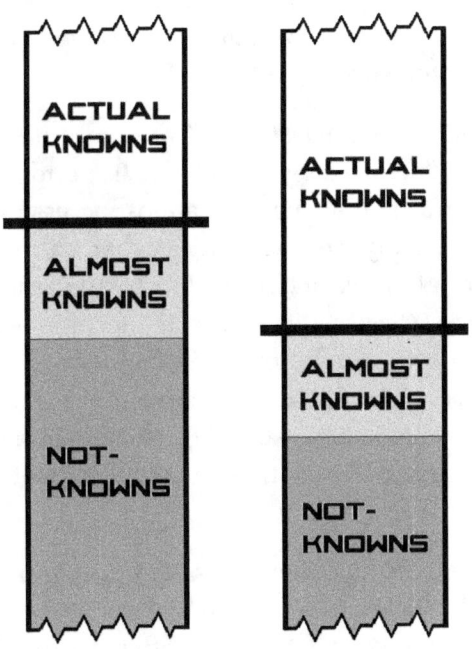

surface" that we do not easily remember (or have any *reality* on)—and these fit our other categories of *almost knowing* and *not-knowing*. The difference between these other two states is how *far* "below-the-surface" a *thing* is.

What you *"almost know"* are those *things* just "below-the-surface"—so *close* to the "surface" that they are almost accessible. This "gray area" includes what an individual is *uncertain* of. With a little assistance (*"Systematic Processing"* techniques), you can actually move a *thing* that is *"almost known"* to an "above-the-surface" state of *"actually knowing"* or remembering again. Only then may it be treated with any *certainty*.

There are also memories very deeply buried "below-the-surface." This includes suppressed data that is not currently accessible—and therefore, presently *"not-known."* Once again, there is a way to move *things* from this state into another state. For this to happen, the previous *"almost known" things* ("just-below-the-surface") need to be "purged" (at least partially) by *"resurfacing"* them into *"actually known" things*.

As more layers of *"almost knowns"* are *resurfaced* into *"actual knowns,"* more of what is *"not-known"* becomes accessible within the "gray area." *Systematic Processing* techniques of *Systemology* are intended to target this "gray area" — promoting increased *realizations* by elevating more knowledge to a state of *Actual Awareness*.

HOW TO STUDY
A SYSTEMOLOGY COURSE

Most *Seekers* study and practice *Systemology* at-a-distance and independent of the

"Mardukite Academy" or any "Master-level" mentors trained therein. This means that the *books* (and to a lesser degree, the *internet*) are the only means of direct contact a *Seeker* maintains with the "Systemology Society" during their studies.

It is quite common to have had negative past experiences with "education" and "learning"—whether in school or other type of instruction. This can sometimes inhibit an individual from pursuing a new *study* later on in their lifetime. However, simply following a few guidelines, ensures a *Seeker's* successful and positive experience when studying this course book—and, of course, the subject of *Systemology* as a whole.

To effectively study and understand a new subject (or a higher gradient of a subject), an individual must be "interested" in the material. A *Seeker* chooses to study *Systemology* because they "want" to, which is to say, on their own "*Self-Determinism.*" While modern society likes to enforce "agreement" (to further solidify a *reality*), a genuine "interest" and true "understanding" can only occur on one's own *Self-Determinism.*

Having established interest, the next *barrier* to understanding is "vocabulary" (words) and "semantics" (meaning). Any specific study, science or tradition is distinguished by the *words* used to communicate it. For true communication to occur, the intended "meaning" for each "word" used must be clearly defined and perfectly understood by the reader or receiver. We call this *"A-for-A"* or *"one-to-one"* communication.

Misunderstood words are the most common reason an individual abandons studying a subject. To relay a proper communication of *Systemology* concepts to a *Seeker*, we use very specific language in our course books. There are newer concepts that more obviously require defining when introduced; and some of our terminology uses familiar words, but with a different or specific meaning than when used elsewhere.

When a misunderstanding occurs, *Awareness* declines. These generally begin to "stack up" after the first occurrence and the level of interest and attention will also decline. This is how a "confusion" develops and the individual will get "bored" with the subject, feel tired, and unable to concentrate.

In extreme cases of confusion, there will be no future interest in studying or "looking at" something further. Feelings of "anger" and "sadness" may result (because one had originally *intended* on knowing something), followed by lower-level opposing "considerations" such as:

"didn't really want to know" or "it probably isn't very good anyways."

The misunderstood word that an individual passed in their study may not be immediately obvious. One solution is to return to the part of the material that was still interesting and enjoyable to read. When scanning around that area of text, there is likely to be a new word (or specific use of a familiar word) that is unclear, but was passed by unnoticed. All *Systemology* books include their own *glossary*. Using this *glossary* and a high-quality dictionary will help resolve this misunderstanding once it is located.

With "interest" and "understanding" secure, the next challenge of learning concerns making a subject *"tangible"* — which means handling it as a *"some-thing"* in the individual's personal *reality* or *Universe*.

Studying intellectual or "philosophical" subjects from a *book* requires excessive amounts of *"thought creation"* — of handling many conceptual images and ideas *"imagined"* solidly in one's "mind" in order to actually "look at" what one is studying. These also require a certain amount of present-time *attention* or *Awareness* to sustain a continual *creation*.

When an individual lacks "objective" examples (objects, graphic representations or direct experience) to examine, they may become "overwhelmed" by "mental-mass" if maintaining too many of their own *images*. This prompts feelings of being "worn out" or "weighed down" — and *considerations* that one "must take a break" or that the subject is "too difficult."

The obvious remedy is to supplement "book-learning" with objective or physical examples. Rather than simply studying or memorizing a series of "dry facts" from an "outside source" (and then returning to "ordinary" life), a student that does understand the material will take it up as their "own" *viewpoint*.

By taking the philosophies up as one's "own" *viewpoint*, the materially is effectively "owned" by the individual. They are not *looking* through a *lens* of someone else. The *"responsibility"* taken by this *ownership* means the freedom to apply information to everyday life and determine the truth of a matter for one's *Self*.

The final *barrier* to learning is the *knowledge* (or "know-*ledge*") itself—the *ledge* or *level* from which a person *knows* or *understands*. A "basic fact" could have many *levels* of potential understanding. To interpret *reality*, an individual "stands" on the *ledge-level* (or *gradient*) of *Knowingness* they have the most "certainty" on.

An effective education of any subject is

27

taught on a *gradient*. This is what is intended by introducing the study of something in "*grades*." Rather than treating a subject as one total mass, true learning is achieved by increasing one's understanding on a *gradual* incline upward. The *ascent* to a mountaintop is not successfully achieved in one leap, but by targeting and reaching specific checkpoints along the way.

In 2019, the "*Grades*" were established for the "Mardukite Academy" to properly indicate what level of understanding a specific book or course is intended for. The entry-point to directly study materials of the Systemology Society at the Academy is "*Grade-III*." Lower *grades* pertain to other *Mardukite* subjects treated separately from Systemology. Higher *grades* continue to explore the "theories and practices" of the Systemology Society as a complete "*Pathway to Ascension*."

This *Basic Course* consists of a series of lessons (booklets) that teach the *"Fundamentals of Systemology."* It is an appropriate entry-point for a new *Systemology* student. It is also applicable to more advanced *Seekers* wanting to increase their *certainty* of understanding at higher *grades* as well.

To study *Systemology* just like a student at the Academy: a *Seeker* reads through all instructional material in a *Basic Course* lesson (booklet) and then performs any practical exercises indicated at the end. Before continuing on to the next lesson (booklet), the material is read again and the light exercises are reapplied.

The second pass through the material is likely to result in different *"realizations"* (an increased *level of understanding*) than the first time. Exercises may seem more vivid or significant. *Seekers* should feel cheerful and confident in their *understan-*

ding of a section (or lesson) before pro-
ceeding even further on *The Pathway*.

YOUR FIRST STEPS ON THE PATHWAY

Systemology is a "holistic" approach to
understanding the human experience. It
is not actually a singular "subject" in itself, but rather, a way to "view" the many
"subjects" of *Life* and all *Existence*. Its
"scope" is not restricted to the rigidly
fixed *considerations* of any one "subject"
exclusively. Yet, for us to properly communicate its specific intended meaning,
Systemology does require its own unique
basic vocabulary.

The "basic vocabulary" and "*Fundamentals*" of *Systemology* are studied together
early on *The Pathway*. They are consistent
for the remaining upper-*grades*. It is our
understanding of them that evolves as we
progress.

The entire structure of *Systemology* rests on foundations of earlier material and earlier researches—such as those found in the earlier *grades* of Mardukite Academy. However, in 2019, new developments made it possible for a *Seeker* to start upon *The Pathway* without first spending years navigating around the pitfalls of other avenues and earlier *grade* subjects. As an extension of the original Academy, the Systemology Society continues to map and define the upper-*grade routes* of our philosophy.

The *Fundamentals of Systemology* are explored throughout the *Basic Course*. The critical foundations of its vocabulary and concepts (from *Grade-II*) were concisely collected in 2019 as an essay—"*Mardukite Zuism: A Brief Introduction.*" It is summarized below to provide a more complete introduction to the "lessons" of the *Basic Course.* Each "lesson" will go on to examine this data in greater detail.

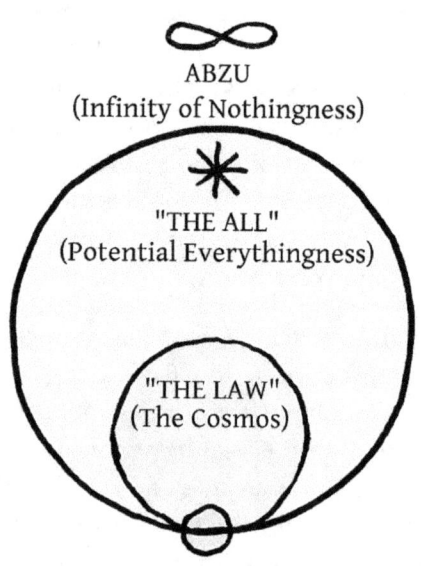

ABZU
(Infinity of Nothingness)

"THE ALL"
(Potential Everythingness)

"THE LAW"
(The Cosmos)

FOUNDATIONS OF SYSTEMOLOGY

Mardukite Zuism is a precursor to *Systemology*. It concerns an intensive archaeological study into the *Arcane Tablets* of Ancient Mesopotamia. Such tablet writings were once used to systematize an understanding of all cosmic knowledge— and they include the Babylonian *Epic of Creation*.

The *Epic of Creation* describes *ALL* ("ANKI") as separated into two *existences*: "AN" and "KI"—literally "heaven" and "earth"—which is to say *"spiritual"* ("AN") and *"physical"* ("KI"). Exterior to, and beyond, the *"potential everythingness"* of all *spiritual* existence and *physical* existence is only an Infinity of Nothingness ("ABZU").

In *Systemology*, we refer to the same two separate states of existence as *"Alpha"*

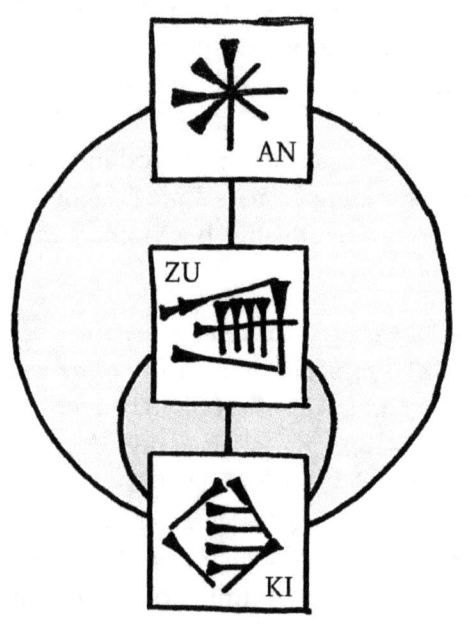

(*spiritual*) and "*Beta*" (*physical*). They are connected only by "*Spiritual Life Awareness*" or "ZU"—a term we have retained in *Systemology* (and for which *Mardukite Zuism* is named). Therefore, we have "*spiritual systems*" and "*physical systems*" connected by "ZU."

The "*Alpha*" *Universe*—of "metaphysical" or "spiritual" energy-matter—is not dependent on the "*Beta*" *Universe* to exist. The two exist independent of one another, except for a single channel or conduit maintaining a connection, which *is* the *Awareness* (the *Spiritual Life-Energy* or "ZU") of an "*Alpha-Spirit*."

"ZU" originates from an "*Alpha*" (*spiritual*) state, separate and distinct from the conditions of "*Beta*" existence that we experience as the *Physical Universe*. "ZU" is *Awareness*—the *Life-Force* or *Thought-Power* that "acts" or "impinges" on an "organism" in *Beta-Existence*.

35

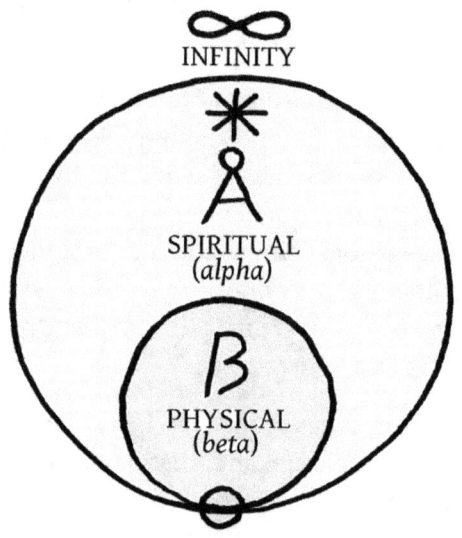

INFINITY

SPIRITUAL
(*alpha*)

PHYSICAL
(*beta*)

For example: the "intention" to read this book, or "commanding" a body to turn a page—those specific components are not actually a part of *this* existence. They are manifestations of a *Spiritual Awareness* (*Alpha*) acting upon an "organic body" (*Beta*). The *"Alpha-Spirit"* is the actual "Eternal" *Self*, which perceives and engages with *Beta-Existence* (*e.g.,* "Life on Earth") by using a "temporary" organic body or *"genetic vehicle."*

The *Alpha-Spirit* engages a *"ZU-Line"*—a *spiritual* "life-line" of *Attention* and *Awareness* ("ZU") energy—to an "organic body" or *genetic-vehicle* in order to directly experience a *"physical" Beta-Existence.*

We use the term *"Self-Honesty"* in *Systemology* to describe the original native *"Alpha"* state of true *Self-Directed* "Beingness" and crystal clear *"Knowingness." Self-Honesty* is the most basic "personality" or

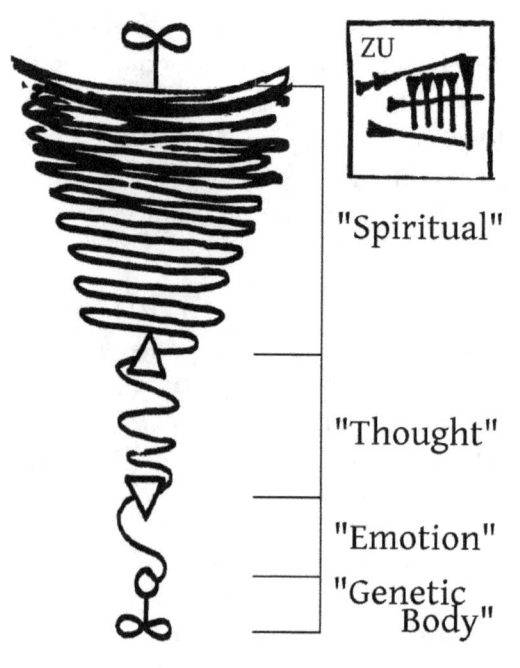

ZU

"Spiritual"

"Thought"

"Emotion"

"Genetic Body"

true expression of *Self* (*Alpha-Spirit*) as "*I-AM*"—a *Self-Determined* state that is *free* of artificial attachments, automatic reaction-response mechanisms, or enforced (*other-determined*) "*reality-agreements*" concerning the Human Condition.

Applying philosophic routes and systematic methods of *Systemology* in order to return *Awareness* of *Self* to its true "*Source*" is referred to as "*The Pathway*." Its structure is based on archaic "models" from the "Ancient Near East" (*Mesopotamia, &tc.*) and elsewhere—such as the "*Chakras*," the Babylonian "*Ladder of Lights*" (*Star-Gates*), and several versions of "*Kabbalah*."

For example: the Mesopotamians built "stepped-pyramids" as temples—called "*ziggurats*"—serving to remind us of the "ZU" bridging the *spiritual* and *physical* systems. Babylonians constructed *ziggurats* to correspond with *seven* primary "steps" or "*Gates*."

39

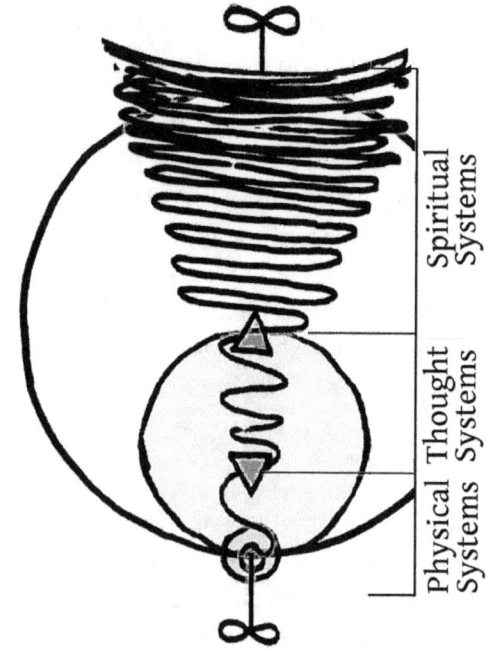

Spiritual Systems

Physical Thought
Systems Systems

The "gradients" or "tiers" of the Babylonian *Ladder of Lights* represent *The Pathway*, because they define the *levels* of *Actualized Awareness* (and *Self-Honesty*)— the states of *Self-purification*—between the "standard-issue" *Human Condition* and *Infinity*. This is the *route* we travel for our "*spiritual defragmentation*" or *Ascension*.

BASIC VOCABULARY REVIEW PUZZLE

ACROSS

3. The standard-issue default manner of filtering perceptions of the Universe, as Self is experiencing it. (2 *words*)

4. The condition of being misaligned, broken apart, shattered, fractured, distorted, or otherwise separated into parts, compared to its original state.

7. A student or practitioner studying and applying Systemology philosophy.

8. The True Self or I-AM Awareness. (2 *words, hyphenated*)

10. The nature of the Physical Universe or material existence.

11. Another way to say "the agreement about what something is."

DOWN

1. The physical body, or any organic life, may serve as your ___. (2 *words*)

2. Regimen or routine of Systemology practices, techniques or exercises that increase Actualized Awareness of Self.

5. Returning to the original native state (or Source of the Spiritual Self) is known universally as ____.

6. A stream of energy connecting Spiritual Awareness to physical existence. (2 *words, hyphenated*)

9. The progressive journey taken in Systemology is referred to as "*The* ___."

LESSON FOUR: ANCIENT SYSTEMOLOGY

LESSON FOUR
WISDOM FROM THE
ARCANE TABLETS

After studying previous lessons (book-lets), a *Seeker* may get to wondering about our interpretation of data drawn from the *Arcane Tablets*; wondering if our presentation of various *models* and *charts* is truly a stable foundation of fundamentals to base our *"Systemology of Everything"* on— if it is something a *Seeker* or student can put their *trust* in as something "solid."

Our philosophy is not one based on *faith* or *dogma*—it is rooted in a *systematized* understanding of some of the most ancient writings found on the planet. While other civilizations may have come and gone in the distant past, these *esoteric* and *hermetic* teachings are those which the "highest minds" based the upper-level systems behind *this* current incarnation of civilization on many thousands of years ago.

If anything, it is *this* information that has actually survived from the even more distant and long-forgotten past. And a perfected communication of it has not yet occurred in modern times prior to our *Systemology*.

The focus of this lesson (booklet)—unlike the previous ones—is not on the explanation of specific topics or subjects. With the previous lessons in mind, or on hand as reference, we take a step further here by delivering the fundamental *"axioms"* (basic principles) of the *Arcane Tablets*— the "raw" data underlying our original research and interpretive models.

Therefore, what follows below are the *essentials* of "Ancient Systemology" that we've carried over into this "New Age." Our knowledge base is otherwise unparalleled in modern *metaphysics* and *esoterica*. We have modernized the language used to now communicate the ancient wisdom set down thousands of years ago.

Much of this data is self-explanatory for a continuing student—providing much for a *Seeker* to study or *reflect* on in view of previous lessons. Individual elements are explained more thoroughly in other lessons, and in the text: "*The Tablets of Destiny Revelation.*" In essence, this is the raw data on which all the former lessons are based. This lesson also collects the sum of this former instruction into a workable *Systemology*.

THE TABLETS OF DESTINY

All data and information is understood as *knowledge* only to the extent or level of *Awareness* that it is *processed*.

"*Understanding*" and *Awareness* have a tendency to "rise and fall" together, building upon one another to form levels on which we base our experience of *Reality*.

The three tiers or levels of processing or understanding include: what is *physically* observed; what is *intellectually* realized; and what is *spiritually* applied.

There are two primary types of knowledge: the "*exoteric*" understanding that is held by the common masses, species or group; and the "*esoteric*" understanding that is restricted to a certain actualized level of *Awareness*.

Self-determinism—the ability to *Self-direct* creation and/or enact change or action— is proportional to one's level of understanding and responsibility.

The ALL ("AN-KI") is the latent unmanifest potential of *Everythingness*.

The LAW—represented on tablets as a "cosmic dragon"—is an existential division between the *Spiritual Universe* ("AN") and the *Physical Universe* ("KI").

This *Cosmic Law* or *Cosmic Ordering* defines the interacting systems of manifestation present in the *Universe—consciousness, motion* and *substance*. It consists of the *reality-agreements* that define the *Physical Universe*.

From an *Alpha* state of existence, *Self* engages with an "organic body" to experience a *Beta* state of existence. *Self* is a "spiritual cause" of "physical effects"—engaging a *Self-Determined* "Will" as *Actualized Awareness*.

The "spiritual energy" transmitted to all *Life* (as "*Lifeforce*") goes by many esoteric names throughout history—but we find the concept first treated as "ZU" on cuneiform tablets from Mesopotamia.

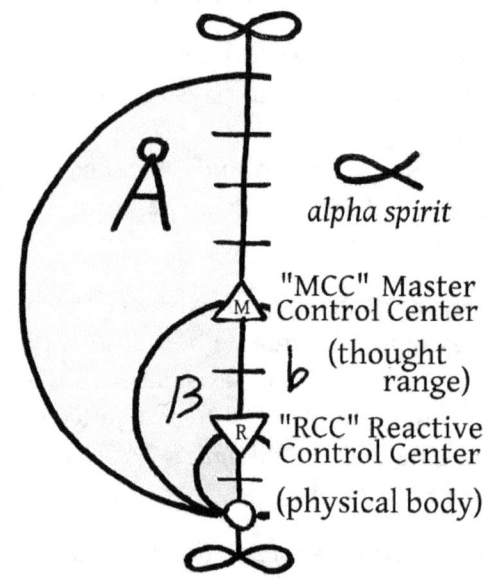

alpha spirit

"MCC" Master Control Center
(thought range)

"RCC" Reactive Control Center
(physical body)

A "conduit channel" of *Spiritual Life Energy* ("ZU") links *Awareness*-levels of our "I-AM-*Self*" from the *Spiritual Universe* (*Alpha*) to the degrees of variation experienced as "*effects*" in the *Physical Universe*.

The term "*levels*" applies best to the relative tiers of personal *Awareness* and understanding regarding *Reality*. These "*levels*" are reflected in the steps of the "ziggurat" temples in ancient Mesopotamia—the original "*Stairway to Heaven*."

The term "*degrees*" is best applied to the *variation* in form and activity perceived by a "*Beta*" state of *Awareness* interior to the *Physical Universe*. This includes "emotional" and "mental" states inherent of the "*Human Condition*."

The "*Self*" is "I" as "*Spirit*" regardless of the position it considers its perspective to be "looking" or "feeling" from. [This true *Alpha* state of *Self* is what some call the "spirit" or "soul."] Both, its *Beingness* and

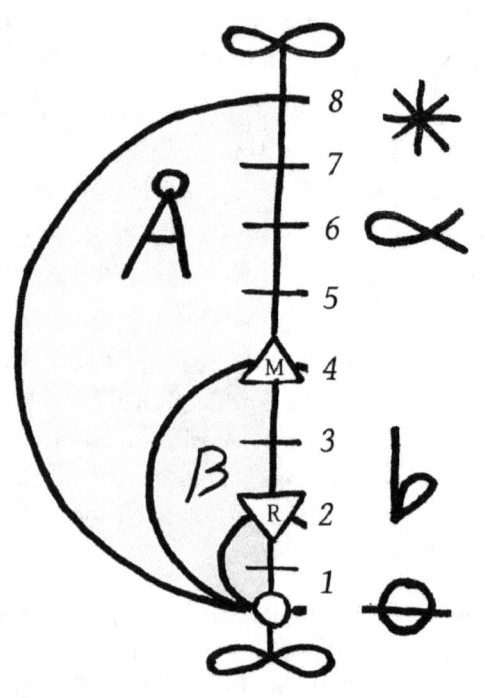

the "conduit channel" of *Spiritual Life Energy* ("ZU") originate from an *Alpha-Existence*, separate and apart from the *Physical Universe*.

It is on this *Lifeline* of "ZU" energy that the *Alpha-Spirit*—operating from the *Spiritual Universe "exterior"* to *Beta-Existence*—is capable of *Self-directing* (*intending*) "thought" into "action" at various degrees of manifestation in the *Physical Universe* (*Beta-Existence*).

ORIGINS OF THE STANDARD MODEL

In *Systemology*, we refer to the continuum or "spiritual conduit" of "ZU" as the "*ZU-Line.*" Using this idea, we may graphically represent "activity" of *Awareness* along an entire "spectrum" of potential ZU "states"—an activity that is generally referred to simply as "*consciou-*

sness" in many other sources and traditions.

When sources mention "states of consciousness" they are referring to various "gradients" of vibration (or frequency) where *Awareness* may be fixed along the *ZU-Line*.

Each "point" or "degree" on the *ZU-Line* has a certain vibration or frequency that defines its "quality." [To establish a *"Standard Model"* we assigned a relative "numeric quantity" to these *degrees* in order to figure a logic of comparison to other *degrees*. Where it pertains to the *"Human Condition"* we refer to it as the *Beta-Awareness Scale* in *"Lesson 1."*]

Graphic representation of frequencies on the *ZU-Line* may include such *degrees* as: a "zero-point" organic *body* (*"genetic-vehicle"*) death; cellular activity and sensory perceptions of the *body*; chemical production induced by *emotion*; *thought* vibrations transmitted between the *Alpha-Spirit* and *"genetic-vehicle."*

There are also points on the *ZU-Line* "exterior" to *Beta-Existence*, where the *Alpha-Spirit* "imagines" and "intends" (uses *Will*). These are *Alpha* qualities that originate from outside of the *Physical Universe*.

We may experience the perspective of any point or *degree* along the entire continuum (*ZU-Line*) from *Self* as the *Alpha-Spirit*. But, the "I-of-the-Observer" remains *Self* in this *Alpha* state, regardless of where *Self* considers its "point-of-view."

Each of us is *knowingly* "projecting" the totality of our *Spiritual Awareness* from an *Alpha* point that is *exterior* to the *Physical Universe*. This "projection" of *Awareness* remains in totality along the *ZU-Line* only to the extent that the "conduit-channel" for *Spiritual Life Awareness* is "clear" of "debris" (*fragmentation*).

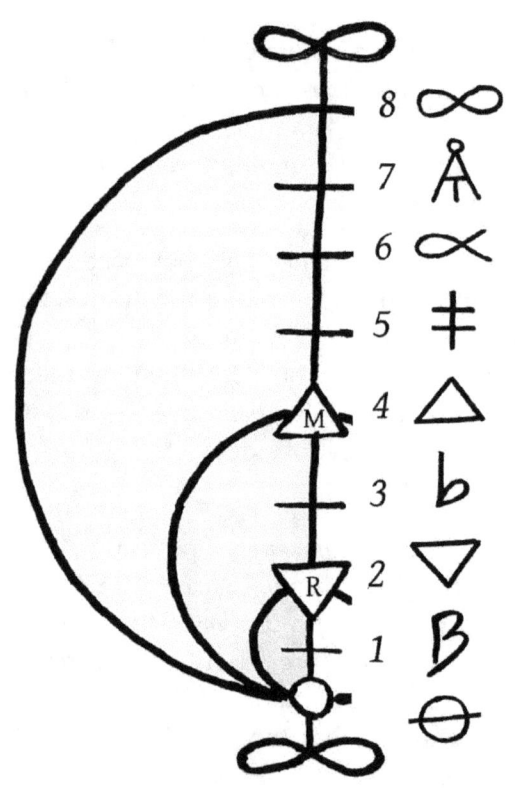

Fragmentation is anything which inhibits the total experience of *Self* as *"Actualized Awareness."* The *"Pathway to Self-Honesty"* in *Systemology* is a personal journey of *clearing* the spiritual-energy *channel*—or *ZU-Line*—of the "debris" *imprinted* upon us by our environments and experiences.

THE PATHWAY TO SELF-HONESTY

Self does not actualize an *Awareness* past a point not understood; our *Awareness* does not surpass our understanding, but it may support a reach toward a higher level of understanding.

When we *defragment* the knowledge-base of our understanding, we remove "dissonance" or else clear the old static beliefs that stand as solid obstacles *fragmenting* the *Awareness* of *Self*.

59

The *process* of *defragmenting Awareness* (on the *"Pathway to Self-Honesty"*) involves closely examining the varying degrees of *fragmented* "thought" and "emotion" fluctuation along the *ZU-Line*.

There are three primary systems that communicate *Life* energy along the *ZU-Line*: spiritual systems, psychological/mind systems and physical systems. These three systems also correlate with the principle systems of manifestation: consciousness, motion, and matter; and also the states of *Self-determinism*: being, doing, and having.

The "peak" level of *Awareness* that we chronically maintain is proportional to the frequency that our attentions and thought-energy is fixed to.

An understanding derived from the *Standard Model* and *ZU-Line* is the basis for "processing" techniques used in *Systemology*—and the map by which we chart our ascent on the *"Pathway to Self-Honesty."*

A holistic examination of *Arcane Tablet* lore revealed two primary communication relay-centers along the *ZU-Line* — both pertaining to the "Mind-System" — acting as an intermediary between the *Alpha-Spirit* and the *genetic-vehicle*. They are not named directly on the original sources, so we titled them for convenience.

The primary *Master-Control-Center* (*MCC*) ["4" on the *Standard Model*] is the direct point-of-contact between the *Alpha* ("spiritual") systems and the Mind-System. It is a perfect computing device to the extent of the information received (and perceived) from "lower levels" of sensory experience.

A secondary *Reactive-Control-Center* ["2" on the *Standard Model*] exists lower on the *ZU-Line*, responsible for discharging emotional *biochemicals* and motor *impulses* of the organic body. It is also quite "impressionable" and stores emotionally-charged information in a form we call *"imprints."*

The *degrees* experienced between "4" and "2" (under the *MCC*) pertain to "states" of thought-involvement with *Beta-Existence.* Those between "2" and "0" (under the *RCC*) pertain to "states" of emotional response.

All sensory input is *perceived* by the Mind-System and communicated back to *Self. Awareness* is communicated along this network of energy relays (along the *ZU-Line*) and forms a "feedback loop" with the *Alpha-Spirit* (*Self*). This activity is what some refer to as *"consciousness."*

If *no* obstruction, distorted *"lens,"* emotional-entanglement or thought-formed solid is *fragmenting* lower-levels of energetic interaction (on the *ZU-Line*), than the actualized *Awareness* an individual experiences is in a condition that we call "*Self-Honesty*."

SYSTEMS OF
THE HUMAN CONDITION

Experience of *Beta-Existence* mainly pertains to our "contact" with energy vibrations carried by everything and everyone we meet. That which is particularly significant concerns communications by family, friends, authority figures, those we admire, and others in our civic communities.

"*Reality*" is an agreement concerning "what *is*" in regards to thought, matter, and the considerations that define our experience. Our experience of *Reality* is either *Self-Determined* or under an "outside" control.

All "systems" are *dynamic* ("variable" and often "interconnected" to other systems) and subject to our participation for us to experience their qualities. The level of this "participation" is subject to our level of understanding and *Awareness*. This is what *is* in our ability to directly control in this lifetime.

Mechanisms of control for *"Reality"* are the same as the control *Self* maintains with other "systems." Short of the *Alpha-Spirit* "creating" a *new* "system," an individual is really only able to *start, stop* or *change* some variable of an existing system—or one system in a network of interconnected systems—such as in the operation of a "vehicle."

The *Standard Model* demonstrates that our thoughts are creating vibrations of varying degrees or frequencies "up and down" the *ZU-Line*. These personal vibrations interact with varying levels or conditions of the "world around us" — and even the "organic body" used to receive environmental stimuli.

Solidified thought-forms and *"Reality-Agreements"* that are intensively broadcast have the tendency to be carried and built upon by others who are affected by them or that in some way "share" in their level of *Reality*.

Even if a person is "opposed to" or "protesting" an *idea*, there is still a "thing" in *Reality*. There is now a "thing" existing for us to *agree* to be in any position about at all. This is an inherent part of "shared" *Reality*.

The *"interior"* (*Beta*) and *"exterior"* (*Alpha*) composition of an individual's *Reality* is treated along the same *ZU-Line* as *Awareness*.

The relay centers of the Mind-System do not perceive a difference between what is generated as a *Reality* "*internally*" within itself from what is sensed as the "*external*" world—nor does *Self*.

We continuously reinforce the *solidity* of our "thought-forms," "imprints," and "fragments," as *Reality* every time we *reactively* or *unknowingly* revisit them with new energy (*attention* or *interest*) and engage an automatic response (that is not *Self-Determined*).

Potentially harmful "*reactive-response*" mechanisms and "*emotional encoding*" may stay dormant in the Mind-System for long periods of time without *resurfacing* (being "restimulated") directly.

Painful memories ("physical" or "emotional"), biological unconsciousness, and other forms of physical trauma, are forms of *fragmentation* that result from having *Awareness* "suspended" for long periods of time (or severe instances) below "2" on the *Standard Model* (ZU-Line). These emo-

tionally encoded *fragmented facets* accu-
mulate as an "energetic-mass"—or "Imprint."

"Imprints" are fixed rigid energy-masses
stored (at the "RCC" level of the Mind-
System) as entangled emotional turbu-
lence, operating "below-the-surface" of
conscious analytical thought.

Using modern *"Systemology Processing"*
techniques, a *Seeker* systematically *"resur-
faces"* and *"confronts"* the content of the
Imprints—thereby freeing up entangled
masses of *Spiritual Life Energy* and increasing actualized *Awareness*.

ARCHAIC AXIOMS

The following *"archaic axioms"* are derived from 20th Century "New Thought"
interpretations of the *Arcane Tablets* that

existed prior to our *Systemology*—and on which our earliest researches were grounded until establishing our own "*Fundamental*" understanding of the *Standard Model* and *ZU-Line*.

The Law *is*. Other than The Law, there is but *Infinity*—which is *Nothingness*. But in that *Infinity of Nothingness*, there is the unmanifest, the latency, the potentiality, the promise of *Manifest Everythingness*.
And the *Nothingness* is counterbalanced by the *Everythingness* of the *Cosmos*.

Under the Law, the *Cosmos* is governed. Each and every thing, and all things, proceed in an "orderly trend"—which is to say "sequentially" and "systematically."

What humans call "*matter*" is the countless centers produced by *Will-Intention* in the *substance principle (system)*, through the action of the *motion principle*.

What is called "*force-energy*" is the action

of the *motion principle (system)* upon the *substance principle (system)*, induced by *Will-Intention*.

"Thought" is the action of *Will-Intention* upon the *consciousness principle (system)*, employing the *substance* and *motion principles* in the operation.

When an individual attains *Self-Actualization* they enter upon the plane (*level*) of *Will-Intention*, and rise up above the plane (*level*) of *"Desire"* (*emotion*).

Will-Intention and *Desire* are "opposing poles" of the same principle (*ZU-Line*), the center or balance of which is *Reason*.

Operating from the plane of *Will-Intention*, one learns to use the *Law* to maintain being at *"Cause"* rather than being passively beneath it as *"Effect."* They may still *create "Desire"* by *Will*—or else, *Will* to *Desire*; but *Will* is no longer being diminished or influenced by *"Desire."* Above this, the individual can learn to *Will* to *Will*.

THE SEVEN COSMIC LAWS

The *Arcane Tablets* reveal that the *Cosmos* is regulated by a "Cosmic Law"—actually *Seven Cosmic Laws*—superimposed over the *Universe*. It constitutes the most basic level of *reality-agreement* concerning experience of manifestation at the level of *Beta-Existence*. An understanding of "Cosmic Law" is inherent in ancient "*Hermetic philosophy*" in addition to "*New Thought*" teachings predating our *Systemology*.

I. *The Law of Orderly Trend.*
"Under this law, there is always manifested law and order in the Cosmos, from suns to atoms; from the highest to the lowest; matter, energy and consciousness."

II. *The Law of Analogy.*
"Under this law, there is found a correspondence and agreement between all of the various forms of manifestation. What is true of the atom, is true of the sun. What is true of matter, is true of energy and mind. To know one is to know all."

III. *The Law of Sequence.*
"Under this law, there is included the activities of what is generally known as 'cause and effect'. Nothing in existence happens by pure chance. Nothing happens without a precedent manifestation, and a subsequent manifestation. Nothing stands alone in exclusion."

IV. *The Law of Rhythm.*
"Under this law falls a variety of phenomena, the most important of which is 'vibration'. Everything in existence is in constant vibration—everything material, mental, or of 'energy'. Upon this fact depends the variety, degrees, states, and

conditions, of the manifestations in the Cosmos. To control vibration is to control all forces in the Universe."

V. *The Law of Balance.*
"Under this law, there is to be found an explanation for the universal equilibrium, compensation, and balance, observed in all manifestation in the Cosmos. One thing balances another; everything has something set opposite it, to balance it."

VI. *The Law of Cyclicity.*
"Under this law is found the cyclic—or circular—trend of all things, physical, mental and spiritual. Everything moves in circular systems. The wise convert the circles into upward spirals. Instead of traveling and endless circle, or downward, the wise rise in spirals to attainment and advancement."

VII. *The Law of Opposites.*
"Under this law is to be found the explanation of the fact that everything has

its opposite; everything *is* and *is-not* at the same time; everything has its *other side*—also the fact that opposite things are alike, in the end, for the extremes meet and contradiction may be reconciled."

PRACTICE EXERCISES

1. Get the sense of making the "body" sit (or lie down) in a comfortable position and in a quiet room (or uninterrupted outdoor environment). Close your eyes and using imagination, *"be outside the body."* Simply shift Awareness to a "point-of-view" just outside the physical body. Using your "exterior" Awareness, gaze upon its form. Even as imaginative practice, this exercise should promote a *realization* that the actual *Awareness* (and true "spiritual" existence) of *Self* is "exterior to" and separate from a body (or genetic-vehicle). Once you have worked with this a while: if you have objection, difficulty, or no reality on this practice, go to *Ex-*

ercise #2; otherwise, go to *Exercise #3*.

2. Certainly a person could object that this is merely *"imaginary"* play—and since one can, in theory, *"imagine anything"* that it really "proves" nothing. Such a *Seeker* might better consider this another way, as the old esoteric instructors once relayed—in trying to *imagine* yourself as "dead." In this wise, all that is generally accessible is the concept of a dead physical body; meanwhile, the actual *Awareness* (of *Self*, the *Alpha-Spirit*) might either "stand" apart from the "dead body" (and be able to view it), or else remain behind to inhabit a "dead body." In either case, what is generally considered *"consciousness"* itself, would not perish or cease at its own level of existence simply be-

cause of the "organic death" of a *genetic-vehicle*.

3. This practice is students that have achieved some sense of *Reality* on the first or second exercise. Focus your *Awareness* (*attention*) on a singular "spot" (or "point") internal to the physical body. You may use your *imagination* to get a "sense" of this "spot" (or "point") —since you won't be able to use the body's "eyes" for that part. Then, focus your *Awareness* (*attention*) on a singular "spot" external to the physical body, in the room (or immediate environment nearby). Get real interested in that "spot" for a moment. Now, fix your attention on the "spot" inside the body; then alternate attention to the "spot" in the room. Once you are proficient in practicing this exercise, continue below.

4. Using the previous exercise as a guideline, practice alternating *Awareness* (*attention*) between "three spots in the body" and "three spots in the room." This may be practiced for two minutes or two hours. The body's "eyes" may be open or closed.

5. Using the previous exercises as a guideline, practice alternating *Awareness* (*attention*) as before, but with *eyes closed*. If necessary, use your *imagination* to get a "sense" of the "spot" in the room —since you now won't be able to use the body's "eyes" for that part either. Of course, practices like these, even if only *imagined*, may "turn on" actual *perception* as if viewing from a point remote from the body. Don't worry if this does not happen immediately—

or even at all—during your first practices.

6. When you are comfortable with the exercises above, practice alternating between "spots in the room" and "spots outside the building." You can begin with eyes open for "spots in the room"—but you will obviously be employing or *imagining* "spirit vision" (or a "remote viewpoint") when looking at "spots outside the building" (or, if outside, looking at "spots" in the surrounding environment that are not visible with the body's "eyes"). At first, just get a "sense" of looking at the "spots" external to the building, just as you did with "spots" internal to the body. With practice, you may find it possible to perceive actual environmental data in this wise.

Continue learning
The Fundamentals of Systemology
in your next
Basic Course
lesson booklet:

**A HISTORY OF SYSTEMOLOGY:
EVOLUTION OF A SPIRITUAL SCIENCE**

GLOSSARY

actualization : to make actual, not just potential; to bring into full solid Reality; to realize fully in *Awareness* as a "thing."

agreement (reality) : unanimity of opinion of what is "thought" to be known; an accepted arrangement of how things are; things we consider as "real" or as an "is" of "reality"; a consensus of what is real as made by standard-issue (common) participants; what an individual contributes to or accepts as "real"; in *Systemology*, a synonym for "*reality.*"

alpha : the first, primary, basic, superior or beginning of some form; in *Systemology*, referring to the state of existence operating on spiritual archetypes and postulates, will and intention "exterior" to the low-level condensation and solidarity of energy and matter as the 'physical universe'.

alpha-spirit : a "spiritual" *Life*-form; the "true" *Self* or I-AM; the *individual*; the spiritual (*alpha*) *Self* that is animating the (*beta*) physical body or "*genetic vehicle*" using a continuous *Lifeline* of spiritual ("*ZU*") energy; an individual spiritual (*alpha*) entity possessing no physical mass or measurable waveform (motion) in the Physical Universe as itself, so it animates the (*beta*) physical body or "*genetic vehicle*" as a catalyst to experience *Self*-determined causality in effect within the *Physical Universe*; a singular unit or point of *Spiritual Awareness* that is *Aware* that it is *Aware.*

alpha thought : the highest spiritual *Self-determination* over creation and existence exercised by an Alpha-Spirit; the Alpha range of pure *Creative Ability* based on direct postulates and considerations of *Beingness*; spiritual qualities comparable to "thought" but originating in Alpha-existence (at "6.0") independently superior to a *beta-anchored* Mind-System, although an Alpha-Spirit may use Will ("5.0") to carry the intentions of a postulate or consideration ("6.0") to the Master Control Center ("4.0").

ascension : actualized *Awareness* elevated to the point of true "spiritual existence" exterior to *beta existence*. An "Ascended Master" is one who has returned to an incarnation on Earth as an inherently *Enlightened One*, demonstrable in their actions—they have the ability to *Self-direct* the "Spirit" as *Self* and maintain consciousness beyond this existence as a personal identity continuum with the same *Self-directed* control and communication of Will-Intention that is exercised, actualized and developed deliberately during one's present incarnation.

associative knowledge : significance or meaning of a facet or aspect assigned to (or considered to have) a direct relationship with another facet; to connect or relate ideas or facets of existence with one another; a reactive-response image, emotion or conception that is suggested by (or directly accompanies) something other than itself; in traditional systems logic, an equivalency of significance or meaning between facets or sets that are grouped together, such as in $(a + b) + c = a + (b + c)$; in NexGen Systemology, erroneous associative knowledge is assignment of the same value to all facets or parts considered as related (even when they are not actually so), such as in $a = a, b = a, c = a$ and so forth without distinction.

attention : active use of *Awareness* toward a specific aspect or thing; the act of "attending" with the presence of *Self*; a direction of focus or concentration of *Awareness* along a particular channel or conduit or toward a particular terminal node or communication termination point; the Self-directed concentration of personal energy as a combination of observation, thought-waves and consideration; focused application of *Self-Directed Awareness*.

awareness : the highest sense of-and-as Self in knowing and being as I-AM (the *Alpha-Spirit*); the extent of beingness directed as a POV experienced by Self as knowingness.

beta (awareness) : all consciousness activity ("*Awareness*") in the "Physical Universe" (KI) or else *beta-existence*; *Awareness* within the range of the *genetic-body*, including material thoughts, emotional responses and physical motors; personal *Awareness* of physical energy and physical matter moving through physical space and experienced as "time"; the *Awareness* held by *Self* that is restricted to a physical organic *Lifeform* or "*genetic vehicle*" in which it experiences causality in the *Physical Universe*.

beta (existence) : all manifestation in the "Physical Universe" (KI); the "Physical" state of existence consisting of vibrations of physical energy and physical matter moving through physical space and experienced as "time"; the conditions of *Awareness* for the *Alpha-spirit* (*Self*) as a physical organic *Lifeform* or "*genetic vehicle*" in which it experiences causality in the *Physical Universe*.

beta-defragmentation : toward a state of *Self-Honesty* in regards to handling experience of the "Physical Universe" (*beta-existence*); an applied spiritual philosophy (or technology) of Self-Actualization

channel : a specific stream, course, current, direction or route; to form or cut a groove or ridge or otherwise guide along a specific course; a direct path; an artificial aqueduct created to connect two water bodies or water or make travel possible.

circuit : a circular path or loop; a closed-path within a system that allows a flow; a pattern or action or wave movement that follows a specific route or potential path only.

condense (condensation) : the transition of vapor to liquid; denoting a change in state to a more substantial or solid condition; leading to a more compact or solid form.

consideration : careful analytical reflection of all aspects; deliberation; determining the significance of a "thing" in relation to similarity or dissimilarity to other "things"; evaluation of facts and importance of certain facts; thorough examination of all aspects related to, or important for, making a decision; the analysis of consequences and estimation of significance when making decisions.

continuity : being a continuous whole; a complete whole or "total round of"; the balance of the equation ["–120" + "120" = "0" &tc.]; an apparent unbroken interconnected coherent whole; also, as applied to Universes in *Systemology*, the lowest base consideration of space-time or commonly shared level of energy-matter apparent in an existence, or else the lowest degree of solidity or condensation whereby all mass that exists is identifiable or communicable with all other mass that exists; represented as "0" on the *Standard Model* for the Physical Universe (*beta-existence*), a level of existence that is below Human emotion, comparable to the solidity of "rocks" and "walls" and "inert bodies."

defragmentation : the *reparation* of wholeness; collecting all dispersed parts to reform an original whole; a process of removing "*fragmentation*" in data or knowledge to provide a clear understanding; applying techniques and processes that promote a *holistic* interconnected *alpha* state, favoring observational *Awareness* of continuity in all spiritual and physical systems; in *Systemology*, a "*Seeker*" achieving an actualized state of basic "*Self-Honest Awareness*" is said to have completed *beta-defragmentation*, whereas *Alpha-defragmentation* is the rehabilitation of the *creative ability*, managing the *Spiri-*

tual Timeline and the POV of *Self* as Alpha-Spirit (I-AM).

existence : the *state* or fact of *apparent manifestation*; the resulting combination of the Principles of Manifestation: consciousness, motion and substance; continued *survival*; that which independently exists.

exterior : outside of; on the outside; in *Systemology*, we mean specifically the POV of *Self* that is *'outside of'* the *Human Condition,* free of the physical and mental trappings of the Physical Universe; a metahuman range of consideration; see also '*Zu-Vision*'.

external : a force coming from outside; information received from outside sources; in *Systemology*, the objective *'Physical Universe'* existence, or *beta-existence*, that the Physical Body or *genetic vehicle* is essentially *anchored* to for its considerations of locational space-time as a dimension or POV.

facets : an aspect, an apparent phase; one of many faces of something; a cut surface on a gem or crystal; in *Systemology*—a single perception or aspect of a memory or "*Imprint*"; any one of many ways in which a memory is recorded; perceptions associated with a painful emotional (sensation) experience and "*imprinted*" onto a metaphoric lens through which to view future similar experiences; other secondary terminals that are associated with a particular terminal, painful event or experience of loss, and which may exhibit the same encoded significance as the activating event.

feedback loop : a complete and continuous circuit flow of energy or information directed as an output from a source to a target which is altered and return back to the source as an input; in *General Systemology*—the continuous process where outputs of a system are routed back as inputs to complete a circuit or loop, which may be closed or connected to other systems/circuits; in *Systemology*—the continuous process where directed *Life* energy and *Awareness* is sent back to *Self* as experience, understanding and memory to complete an energetic circuit as a loop.

fragmentation : breaking into parts and scattering the pieces; the *fractioning* of wholeness or the *fracture* of a holistic interconnected *alpha* state, favoring observational *Awareness* of perceived connectivity between parts; *discontinuity*; separation of a totality into parts; in *Systemology*, a person outside a state of *Self-Honesty* is said to be *fragmented*.

genetic-vehicle : a physical *Life*-form; the physical (*beta*) body that is animated/controlled by the (*Alpha*) *Spirit* using a continuous *Lifeline* (ZU); a physical (*beta*) organic receptacle and catalyst for the (*Alpha*) *Self* to operate "causes" and experience "effects" within the *Physical Universe*.

gradient : a degree of partitioned ascent or descent along some scale, elevation or incline; "higher" and "lower" values in relation to one another.

holistic : the examination of interconnected systems as encompassing something greater than the *sum* of their "parts."

imagination : the ability to create *mental imagery* in one's Personal Universe at will and change or alter it as desired; the ability to create, change and dissolve mental images on command or as an act of will; to create a mental image or have associated imagery displayed (or "conjured") in the mind that may or may not be treated as real (or memory recall) and may or may not accurately duplicate objective reality; to employ *creative abilities* of the Spirit that are independent of reality agreements with beta-existence.

intention : directed application of Will; to intend (have "in Mind") or signify (give "significance" to) for or toward a particular purpose; in *Systemology* (from the *Standard Model*)—the spiritual activity at WILL (5.0) directed by an *Alpha Spirit* (7.0); the application of WILL as "Cause" from a higher order of Alpha Thought and consideration (6.0).

interior : inside of; on the inside; in *Systemology*, we mean specifically the POV of *Self* that is fixed to the *'internal' Human Condition*, including the *Reactive Control Center* (RCC) and Mind-System or *Master Control Center* (MCC); within *beta-existence*.

internal : a force coming from inside; information received from inside sources; in *Systemology*, the objective experience of *beta-existence* associated with the Physical Body or *genetic vehicle* and its POV regarding sensation and perception; from inside the body; in the body.

Human Condition : a standard default state of Human experience, generally accepted to be the extent of its potential identity (*beingness*).

imprint : to strongly impress, stamp, mark (or outline) onto a softer 'impressible' substance; to mark with pressure onto a surface; in *Systemology*, used to indicate permanent Reality impressions marked by frequencies, energies or interactions experienced during periods of emotional distress, pain, unconsciousness, loss, enforcement, or something antagonistic to physical (personal) survival, all of which are are stored with other reactive response-mechanisms at lower-levels of *Awareness* as opposed to the active memory database and proactive processing center of the Mind; an experiential "memory-set" that may later resurface—be triggered or stimulated artificially—as Reality, of which similar responses will be engaged automatically; holographic-like imagery "stamped" onto consciousness as composed of energetic *facets* tied to the "snap-shot" of an experience.

imprinting incident : the first or original event instance communicated and *emotionally encoded* onto an individual's "*Spiritual Timeline*" (recorded memory from all lifetimes), which formed a permanent impression that is later used to mechanistically treat future contact on that channel; the first or original occurrence of some particular *facet* or mental image related to a certain type of *encoded response*, such as pain and discomfort, losses and victimization, and even the acts that we have taken against others along the *Spiritual Timeline* of our existence that caused them to also be *Imprinted*.

knowledge : clear personal processing of informed understanding; information (data) that is actualized as effectively workable understanding; a demonstrable understanding on which we may 'set' our *Awareness*—or literally a "know-ledge."

Master-Control-Center (MCC) : a perfect computing device to the extent of the information received from "lower levels" of sensory experience/perception; the proactive communication system of the "*Mind*"; a relay point of active *Awareness* along the Identity's *ZU-line*, which is responsible for maintaining basic *Self-Honest* clarity of *Knowingness* as a *seat of consciousness* between the *Alpha-Spirit* and the secondary "*Reactive Control Center*" of a *Lifeform* in *beta existence*; the Mind-center for an *Alpha-Spirit* to actualize cause in the *beta existence*; the analytical *Self-Determined* Mind-center of an *Alpha-Spirit used* to project *Will* toward the genetic body; the point of contact between *Spiritual Systems* and the *beta existence*; presumably the "*Third Eye*" of a being connected directly to the *I-AM-Self*, which is responsible for *determining* Reality at any time; in *Systemology*, this is plotted at (4.0) on the continuity model of the *ZU-line*.

mental image : a subjectively experienced "picture" created and imagined into being by the Alpha-Spirit (or at lower levels, one of its automated mechanisms) that includes all perceptible *facets* of totally immersive scene, which may be forms originated by an individual, or a "facsimile-copy" ("snap-shot") of something seen or encountered; a duplication of wave-forms in one's Personal Universe as a "picture" that mirror an "external" Universe experience, such as an *Imprint*.

perception : internalized processing of data received by the *senses*; to become *Aware of* via the senses.

point-of-view (POV) : a point to view from; an opinion or attitude as expressed from a specific identity-phase; a specific standpoint or vantage-point; a definitive manner of consideration specific to an individual phase or identity; a place or position affording a specific view or vantage; circumstances and programming of an individual that is conducive to a particular response, consideration or belief-set (paradigm); a position (consideration) or place (location) that provides a specific view or perspective (subjective) on experience (of the objective). May also be referred to in our texts as a "*viewpoint.*"

processing, systematic : the inner-workings or "through-put" result of systems; in *Systemology*, a methodology of applied spiritual technology used toward personal Self-Actualization; methods of selective directed attention, communicated language and associative imagery that targets an increase in personal control of the human condition.

reactive control center (RCC) : the secondary (reactive) communication system of the "*Mind*"; a relay point of *Awareness* along the Identity's *ZU-line*, which is responsible for engaging basic motors, biochemical processes and any *programmed automated responses* of a living *beta* organism; the reactive Mind-Center of a living organism relaying communications of *Awareness* between causal experience of *Physical Systems* and the "*Master Control Center*"; it presumably stores all emotional encoded imprints as fragmentation of *ZU* (within the range of the "*psychological/ emotive systems*" of a being), which it may *react* to as Reality at any time; in *Systemology*, this is plotted at (2.0) on the continuity model of the *ZU-line*.

reality : see "*agreement.*"

Seeker : an individual on the *Pathway to Self-Honesty*; a practitioner of *Mardukite Systemology* or *Systemology Processing* that is working toward *Spiritual Ascension*.

Self-actualization : bringing the full potential of the Human spirit into Reality; expressing full capabilities and creativeness of the *Alpha-Spirit*.

Self-determinism : the freedom to act, clear of external control or influence; the personal control of Will to direct intention.

Self-honesty : the basic or original *alpha* state of *being* and *knowing*; clear and present total *Awareness* of-and-as *Self*, in its most basic and true proactive expression of itself as *Spirit* or *I-AM*—free of artificial attachments, perceptive filters and other emotionally-reactive or mentally-conditioned programming imposed on the human condition by the systematized physical world; the ability to experience existence without judgment.

sensation : an external stimulus received by internal sense organs (receptors/sensors); sense impressions.

slate : a hard thin flat surface material used for writing on; a chalk-board, which is a large version of the original wood-framed writing slate, named for the rock-type it was made from.

Spheres of Existence (dynamic systems) : a model of *eight* concentric circles, rings or spheres (each larger than the former) that is overlaid onto the Standard Model of Beta-Existence to demonstrate dynamic systems of existence extending out from a POV of Self (often as a "body") at the *First Sphere*; these are given as a basic eightfold system: *Self*, *Home/Family*, *Groups*, *Humanity*, *Life on Earth*, *Physical Universe*, *Spiritual Universe* and *Infinity-Divinity*.

spiritual timeline : a continuous stream of moment-to-moment *Mental Images* (or a record of experiences) that defines the "past" of a spiritual being (or *Alpha-Spirit*) and which includes impressions (*imprints, &tc.*) form all life-incarnations and significant spiritual events the being has encountered.

Standard Model, The (systemology) : our existential and cosmological *standard model* or cabbalistic model; a "*monistic continuity model*" demonstrating *total system* interconnectivity "above" and "below" observation of any apparent *parameters*; the original presentation of the *ZU-line*, represented as a singular vertical (y-axis) waveform in space across dimensional levels or Universes (*Spheres of Existence*) without charting any specific movement across a dimensional time-graph x-axis; The Standard Model of Systemology represents the basic workable synthesis of common denominators in models explored throughout Grade-I and Grade-II material.

system : from the Greek, "to set together"; to set or arrange things or data together so as to form an orderly understanding of a "whole."

terminal (node) : a point, end or mass on a line; a point or connection for closing an electric circuit, such as a post on a battery terminating at each end of its own systematic function; any end point or 'termination' on a line; a point of connectivity with other points; in systems, any point which may be treated as a contact point of interaction; anything that may be distinguished as an 'is' and is therefore a 'termination point' of a system or along a flow-line which may interact with other related systems it shares a line with; a point of interaction with other points.

thought-form : apparent *manifestation* or existential *realization* of *Thought-waves* as "solids" even when only apparent in Reality-agreements of the Observer; the treatment of *Thought-waves* as permanent *imprints* obscuring *Self-Honest* clarity of *Awareness* when reinforced by emotional experience as actualized "thought-formed solids" ("*beliefs*") in the Mind; energetic patterns that "surround" the individual.

ZU : the ancient Sumerian cuneiform sign for the archaic verb—"*to know,*" "*knowingness*" or "*awareness*"; in *Mardukite Zuism and Systemology*, the active energy/matter of the "Spiritual Universe" (AN) experienced as a *Lifeforce* or *consciousness* that imbues living forms extant in the "Physical Universe" (KI); "*Spiritual Life Energy*"; energy demonstrated by the WILL of an actualized *Alpha-Spirit* in the "Spiritual Universe" (AN), which impinges its *Awareness* into the Physical Universe (KI), animating/controlling *Life* for its experience of *beta-existence* along an individual Alpha-Spirit's personal *Identity-continuum*, called a *ZU-line*.

Zu-Line : a theoretical construct in *Mardukite Zuism and Systemology* demonstrating *Spiritual Life Energy* (*ZU*) as a personal individual "continuum" of Awareness interacting with all Spheres of Existence on the Standard Model of Systemology; a spectrum of potential variations and interactions of a monistic continuum or singular *Spiritual Life Energy (ZU)* demonstrated on the Standard Model; an energetic channel of potential POV and "locations" of Beingness, demonstrated in early Systemology materials as an individual Alpha-Spirit's personal *Identity-continuum*, potentially connecting *Awareness (ZU)* of *Self* with "*Infinity*" simultaneous with all points considered in existence; a symbolic demonstration of the "*Life-line*" on which *Awareness (ZU)* extends from the direction of the "Spiritual Universe" (AN) in its true original *alpha state* through an entire possible range of activity resulting in its *beta state* and control of a *genetic-entity* occupying the *Physical Universe (KI)*.

THE SYSTEMOL

Seekers and students of the *Basic Course* and *Professional Course* will also be interested in the *Advanced Series* of the *Systemology Core*. These volumes are a complete chronological record of the Mardukite New Thought developments from the Systemology Society, published in 2019 through 2023.

The *Systemology Core* begins with the first professional publication released when the *Mardukite Systemology Society* emerged from the underground in 2019, with: *"The Tablets of Destiny Revelation."*

OGY PATHWAY

The Tablets of Destiny Revelation:
*How Long-Lost Anunnaki Wisdom
Can Change the Fate of Humanity*

Crystal Clear: *Handbook for Seekers*

Metahuman Destinations (*2 volumes*)

Imaginomicon:
Approaching Gateways to Higher Universes

Way of the Wizard: *Utilitarian Systemology*

Systemology-180: *Fast-Track to Ascension*

Systemology Backtrack:
Reclaiming Spiritual Power & Past-Life Memory

PUBLISHED BY THE **JOSHUA FREE** IMPRINT REPRESENTING

The Mardukite Academy of Systemology

mardukite.com

www.ingramcontent.com/pod-product-compliance
Lightning Source LLC
Chambersburg PA
CBHW071209120626
46546CB00006B/2487